Dear Anxiety

Thank you for visiting, but I'm going to ask you to leave!

Written by

D. Prudhomme

DORRANCE PUBLISHING CO
EST. 1920
PITTSBURGH, PENNSYLVANIA 15238

The contents of this work, including, but not limited to, the accuracy of events, people, and places depicted; opinions expressed; permission to use previously published materials included; and any advice given or actions advocated are solely the responsibility of the author, who assumes all liability for said work and indemnifies the publisher against any claims stemming from publication of the work.

All Rights Reserved
Copyright © 2024 by D. Prudhomme

No part of this book may be reproduced or transmitted, downloaded, distributed, reverse engineered, or stored in or introduced into any information storage and retrieval system, in any form or by any means, including photocopying and recording, whether electronic or mechanical, now known or hereinafter invented without permission in writing from the publisher.

Dorrance Publishing Co
585 Alpha Drive
Pittsburgh, PA 15238
Visit our website at www.dorrancebookstore.com

ISBN: 979-8-89127-877-6
eISBN: 979-8-89127-375-7

Dedicated to

Kee

Having you in my life has made me a better person.
You have changed my view of the world, have been my best teacher and you have taught me more than you'll ever know.
I love you with all my heart!

Buzz off

Dear Anxiety,

Listen up! I know I need you. You keep me alert to dangers in the world around me. I get it! It's about being human, but you stay WAY TOO LONG! It doesn't feel good when you're with me, so I'm going to ask you to buzz off!

> You despise when I visit for too long?

Take A Hike

I've realized when you visit that my heart races. It beats incredibly fast, and that makes me worry a lot. I swear it even skips a beat! Your alertness is noted and appreciated, but I'm going to ask you to take a hike.

Hmm. I don't think my presence is worrisome.

Bug Out

I get sweaty sometimes when you drop by. My temperature rises like hot lava exploding from a volcano! That's not the best feeling either. You're very vigilant, but I'm going to ask you to bug out.

I must be powerful if I make you sweat!

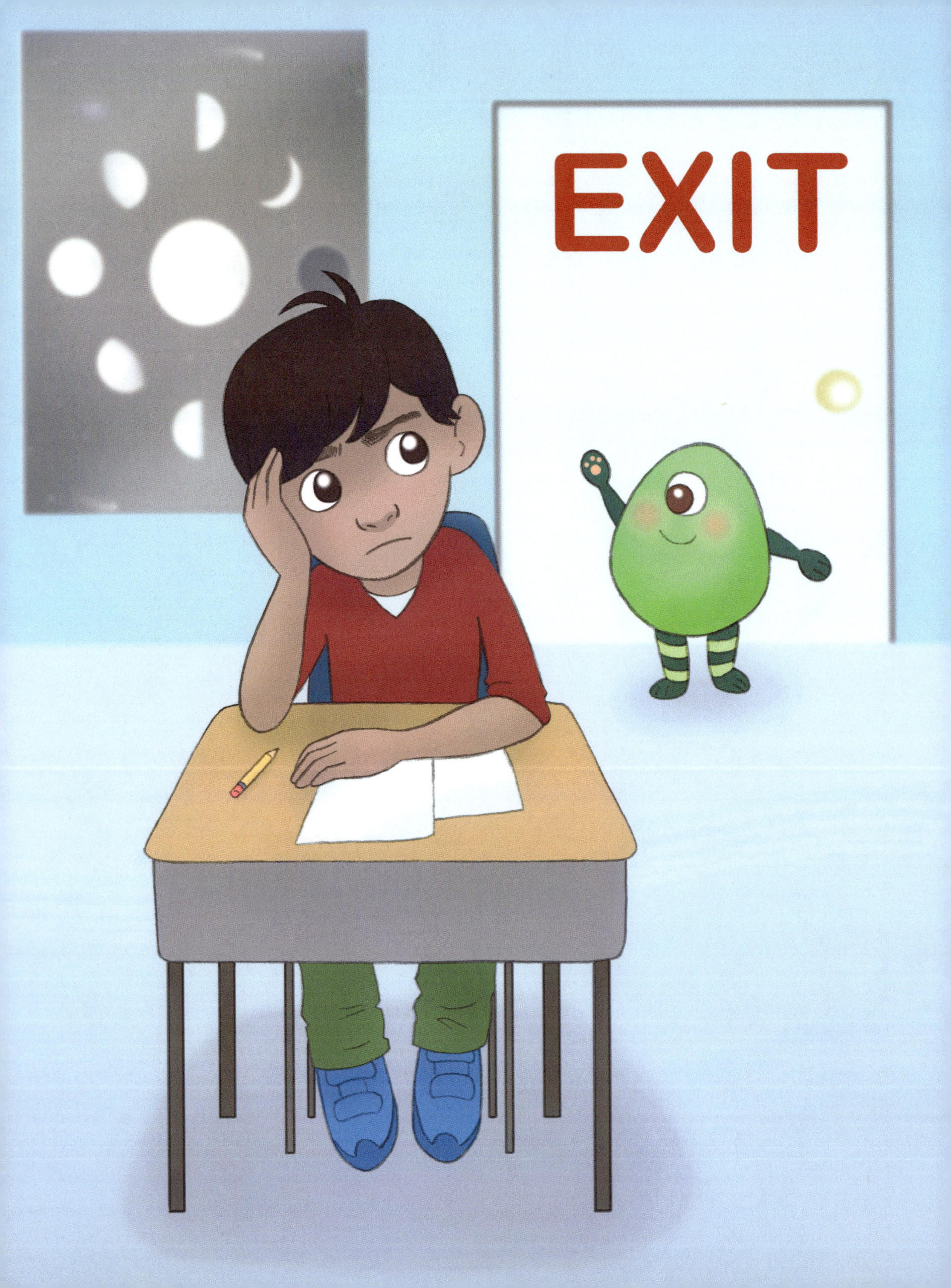
EXIT

Once in a while when you drop in, I have A LOT of trouble focusing. That becomes frustrating, especially when I'm in school. Again, your presence is appreciated, but I'm going to ask you to find the exit!

You can't possibly think I'm hindering your day?

Skedaddle

Believe it or not, every so often I start breathing really heavily, and I get this nervous feeling inside my body when you show up. I'm as tense as a mouse surrounded by cats, so I'm going to ask you to skedaddle.

What?
I create tension for you?

Show you to the door

Anxiety, you even make me shake and feel weak when you come by. Strange, uncomfortable feelings start showing up in my belly. I see you and feel your arrival. However, I do not like these peculiar feelings, so, I'm going to show you to the door!

I didn't realize I caused so much discomfort.

Hit the Road

When you hang around at bedtime, I have trouble sleeping. I toss and turn and my mind races. About a billion thoughts bebop in and out. Why do you visit when I'm trying to relax? When I want to hit the hay, I'm going to ask you to hit the road!

You don't want me nearby at bed time?

Vamoose   Take Off
Scat

I've also noticed that you like to show up when I'm trying something new. You pop into my brain to convince me not to attempt new things. WHY do you do that? It's so annoying! I'd like to join fun and exciting activities, so I'm going to ask you to vamoose, scat, take off!

Are you implying that I'm not being helpful?

Vacate

You know, there are times when you actually make me dizzy and even nauseous. Ugh… it feels awful inside! Anxiety, I'm just tired of you trying to control me. You need to vacate the premises!

I'm beginning to feel like a nuisance.

Just Leave

Okay. Listen up, you belly rumbling, heavy breathing, distracting bully! I'll acknowledge you and even thank you on some occasions, but don't overstay your welcome. You do that WAY TOO OFTEN. Just leave when I give you the sign!

Perhaps I have been lingering for too long.

head out

gone

run along

adios

Anxiety, here's the plan. When I take some deep breaths and release them SLOWLY, that means you need to head out!

If you hear me counting to ten, I want you GONE by the time I utter ten!

Sometimes, I'll choose to focus on my five senses. When you feel me doing that, it's time for you to run along.

By the way, I might even add some exercise to my day just to get rid of you. I'm not allowing you to take over my body and mind anymore. Adios, anxiety!

It's time for me to go.

When anxiety visits me, my plan is to...

Pay attention to your body when you become nervous about an event. What part of your body is affected? Circle or highlight it below.

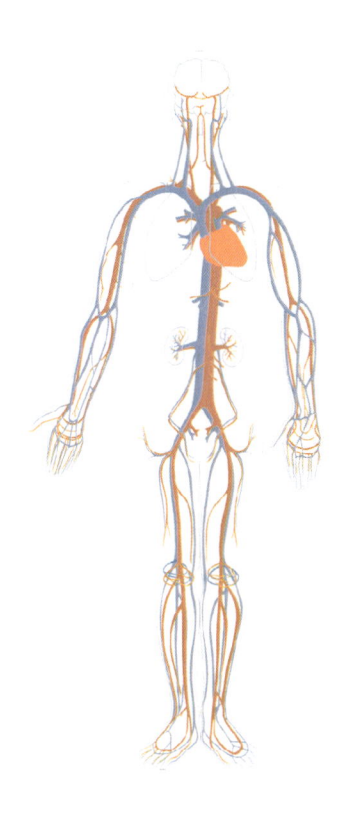

Try to describe in words how the area you highlighted or circled feels.

_____
_____
_____

Write or draw all your worries in the cloud below.
Use color, cursive, print, or anything to be creative.
Then, imagine all your worries floating away.

Write a letter to your biggest fear. Tell the fear why you no longer want it around. Give several great reasons.

Brainstorm a list of strategies to use when you are feeling anxious.

My BIGGEST worries!

Write your 4 biggest worries anywhere in the diagram below.

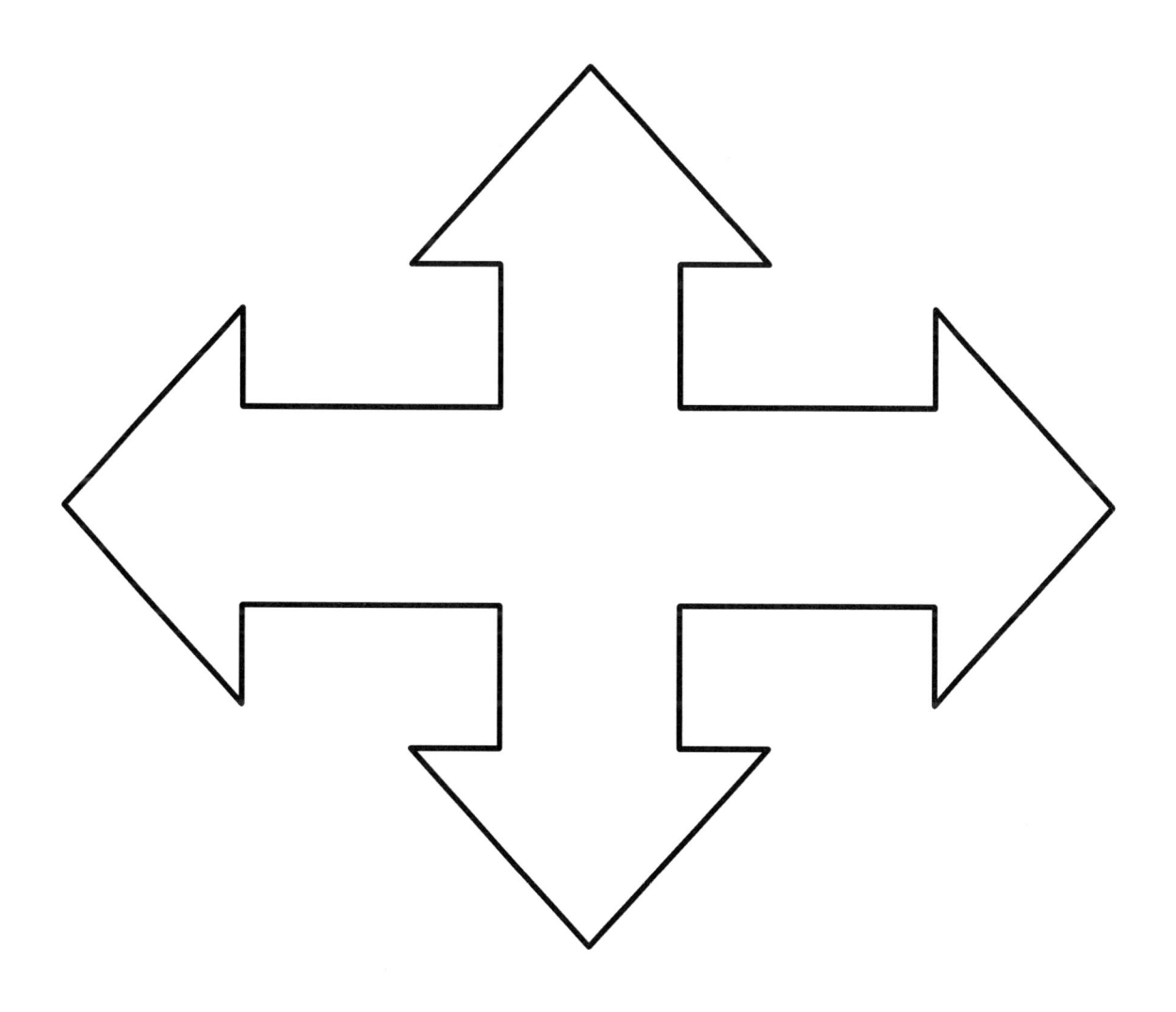

About the Author

Debra Prudhomme is a voice for children. She has been an educator for over 20 years and gives presentations regarding the social, emotional and behavioral health of our youth and on suicide awareness. She has a BS degree in Elementary Education and English from Bridgewater State University. She is also a veteran. After 20 years in the classroom, she has witnessed first hand the upswing in children's anxiety, depression, and so much more. This book is her way of giving children and families another tool to openly discuss anxiety. Reach out to her anytime. Find her website at, becuriouskids.com.

Schedule an author visit at your school or facility.
deb.becurious@gmail.com